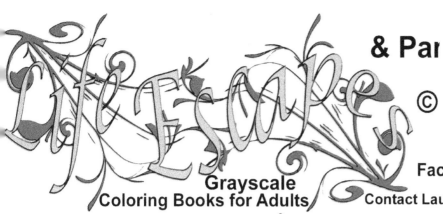 

& Par

© Laura Kilgore

Twitter @colorpagefree
Facebook @lifeescapescoloringbooks
Contact Laura kilgore7098@gmail.com

http://coloringbooksforadults.shop

You may make copies of the pages in this book for your personal use only. Commercial use, giving away and/or posting online of the uncolored images as they appear in this book is not permitted.

THIS IS A GRAYSCALE ADULT COLORING BOOK

Grayscale is very different than standard coloring books. It is designed for those who wish to create realistic colored images.

We have included coloring tips and instructions in the back of the book.

Visit http://coloringbooksforadults.shop for

1. Downloadable grayscale coloring books by Life Escapes designers
2. Download free color guides
3. NEW! How to color grayscale video tutorials
4. Free grayscale basics videos
5. Free grayscale coloring pages
6. 3 piece coloring greating card sets
7. 10 piece sampler packs

All Life Escapes Adult Coloring Books are available for purchase in

PDF digital format on our website. Just visit

https://coloringbooksforadults.shop   Sign up for our newsletter

to get 50% off all downloadable books and sampler packs for life

for Inquiries not regarding artwork
Contact Kimberly: life.escapes.series@gmail.com

https://coloringbooksforadults.shop

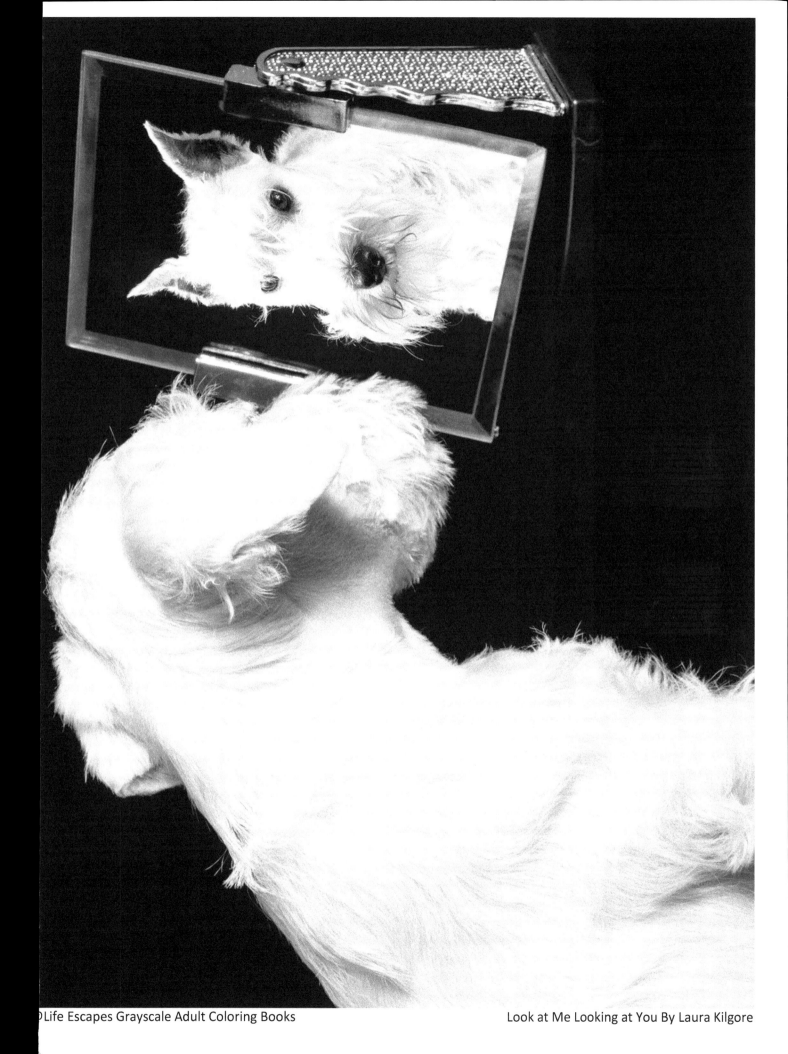

Life Escapes Grayscale Adult Coloring Books — Look at Me Looking at You By Laura Kilgore

https://coloringbooksforadults.shop

https://coloringbooksforadults.shop

https://coloringbooksforadults.shop

https://coloringbooksforadults.shop

©Life Escapes Grayscale Adult Coloring Books — Look at Me Looking at You By Laura Kilgore

https://coloringbooksforadults.shop

https://coloringbooksforadults.shop

https://coloringbooksforadults.shop

@Life Escapes Grayscale Adult Coloring Books — Look at Me Looking at You By Laura Kilgore

https://coloringbooksforadults.shop

https://coloringbooksforadults.shop

https://coloringbooksforadults.shop

https://coloringbooksforadults.shop

https://coloringbooksforadults.shop

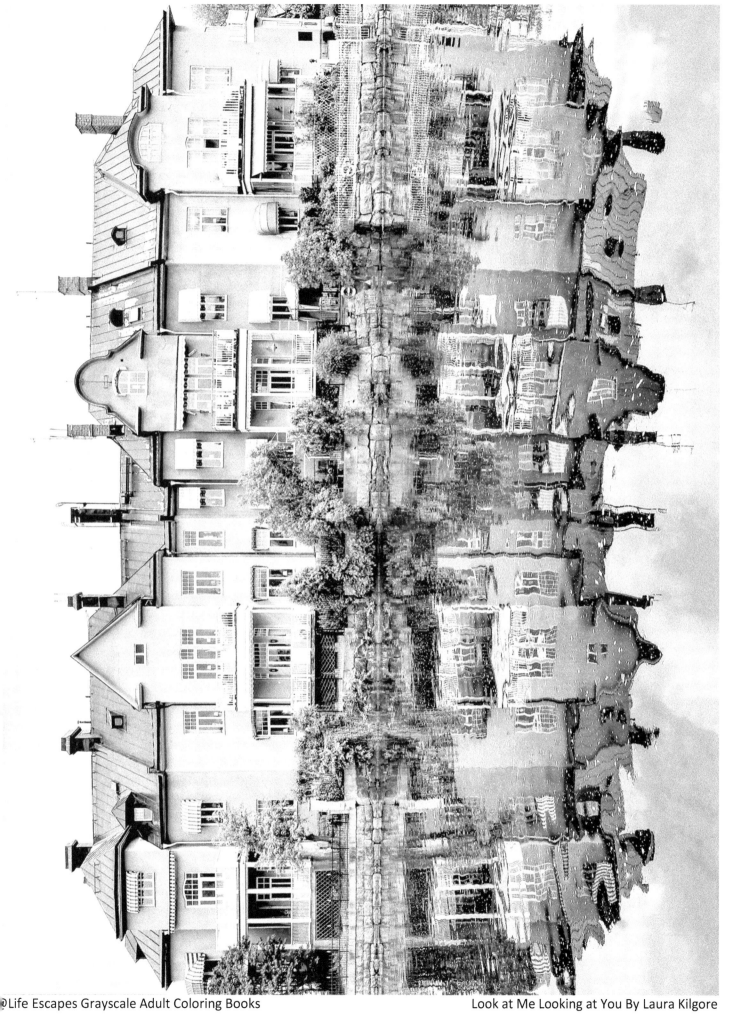

https://coloringbooksforadults.shop

https://coloringbooksforadults.shop

https://coloringbooksforadults.shop

https://coloringbooksforadults.shop

https://coloringbooksforadults.shop

https://coloringbooksforadults.shop

https://coloringbooksforadults.shop

https://coloringbooksforadults.shop

https://coloringbooksforadults.shop

https://coloringbooksforadults.shop

https://coloringbooksforadults.shop

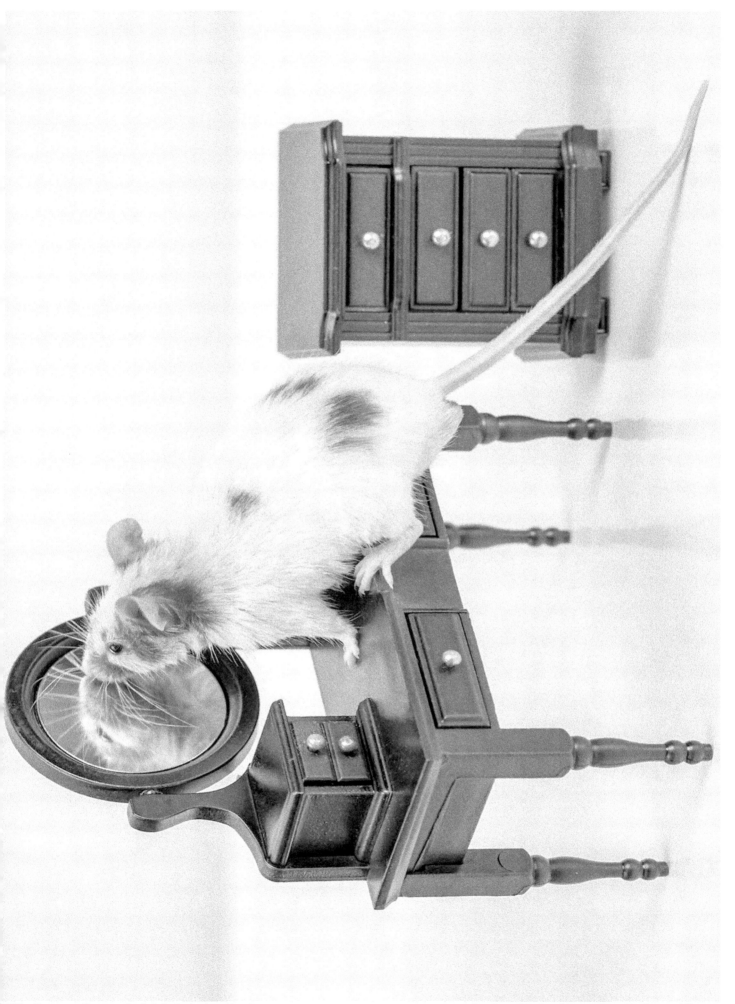

https://coloringbooksforadults.shop

https://coloringbooksforadults.shop

https://coloringbooksforadults.shop

https://coloringbooksforadults.shop

https://coloringbooksforadults.shop

https://coloringbooksforadults.shop

https://coloringbooksforadults.shop

Look at Me Looking at You By Laura Kilgore

https://coloringbooksforadults.shop

https://coloringbooksforadults.shop

https://coloringbooksforadults.shop

https://coloringbooksforadults.shop

https://coloringbooksforadults.shop

https://coloringbooksforadults.shop

https://coloringbooksforadults.shop

https://coloringbooksforadults.shop

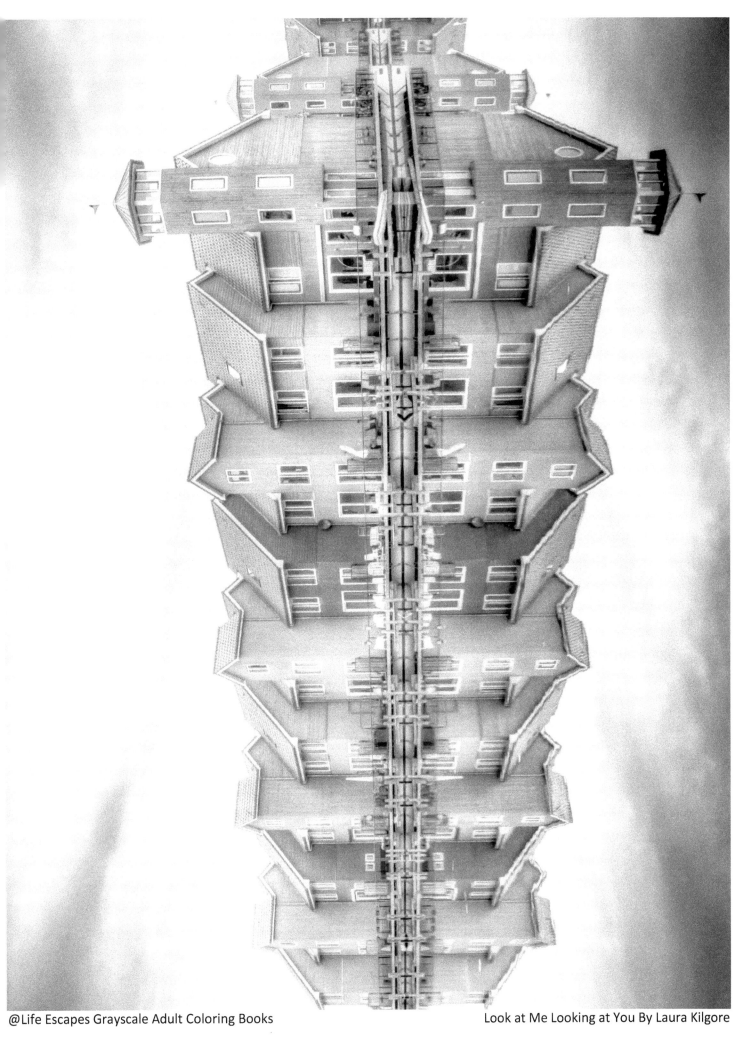

https://coloringbooksforadults.shop

https://coloringbooksforadults.shop

https://coloringbooksforadults.shop

https://coloringbooksforadults.shop

https://coloringbooksforadults.shop

https://coloringbooksforadults.shop

COLOR TEST PAGE

@Life Escapes Grayscale Adult Coloring Books

Look at Me Looking at You By Laura Kilgore

https://coloringbooksforadults.shop
How to get your FREE color guide

As of April 1, 2020 we no longer honor our free pdf with amazon purchase. You may continue to download the free color guide for all our books on our website. Here is how to do it.

1. Go to https://coloringbooksforadults.shop
2. Click on top menu button that says full pdf library
3. Find the cover pic of your book and click on it
4. Scroll down to the color guide section and click the button to download the color guide

Introducing...

How to color grayscale video tutorials for sale on our website.

Watch our Basics Series Free

Go to the site address at the top then click on the "How to Color Grayscale" button in the top menu

Still Need Help?

life.escapes.series@gmail.com

https://coloringbooksforadults.shop

Basic Grayscale Coloring Instructions

Step 1 - Choose an object in the coloring page to start with then you will need black, white and light, medium & dark shades of the color you choose. (Examples: a tree, an animal, a flower etc...)

Step 2 - With your color pencils, coloring in a circular motion, color white and light gray areas with your light color. Color dark grays with your dark color. Color medium grays with your medium color.

Tip: Overlap medium color a little ways into the light and dark areas for a seamless blend of your colors.

Step 3 - If you color with a light hand, add more layers of color to make it more visible or vibrant. Then on the highlight areas, add white over the area. Use black to outline and enhance the very darkest areas.

Tip: Keep your pencils sharp and color in a circular motion. If you have a heavy hand, move your fingers higher up on the pencil to ensure you are coloring lightly when needed.

For further techniques, methods, mediums, tips and tricks, check out our all new video tutorials on our website.

Go to https://coloringbooksforadults.shop

Then click on "How to Color Grayscale" button in the top menu

Our videos on the basics are free to watch

We want you to enjoy your coloring experience

If you are struggling with an image, please go to http://coloringbooksforadults.shop to download the color guide for this book. You will also find videos on how to color grayscale. If you still need assistance, please email Kimberly at life.escapes.series@gmail.com

Follow us on Facebook @lifeescapescoloringbooks

Adult Coloring Books
http://coloringbooksforadults.shop
life.escapes.series@gmail.com

You might also enjoy adult coloring books from our partners

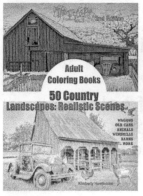    

 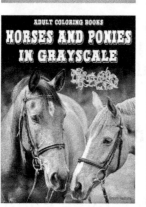   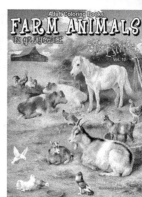

   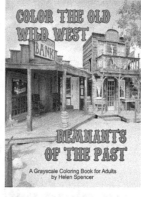 

  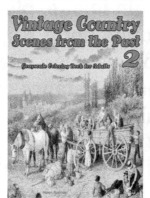  

https://coloringbooksforadults.shop

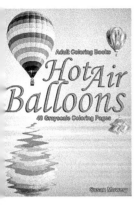
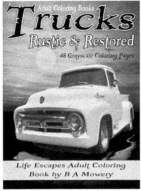

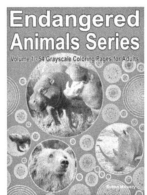
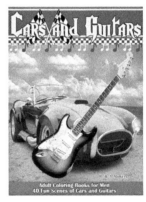

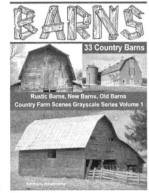
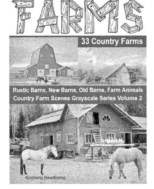

@Life Escapes Grayscale Adult Coloring Books   Look at Me Looking at You By Laura Kilgore

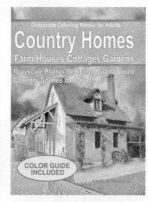

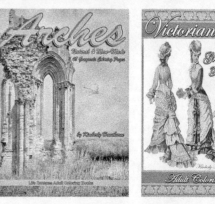

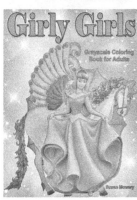

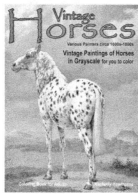

https://coloringbooksforadults.shop

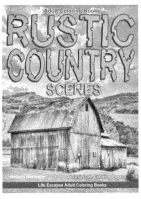

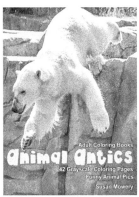
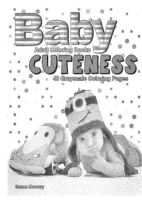

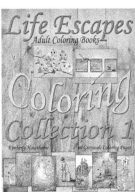

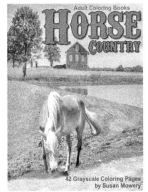
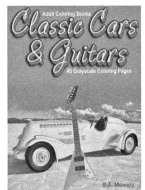

@Life Escapes Grayscale Adult Coloring Books   Look at Me Looking at You By Laura Kilgore

https://coloringbooksforadults.shop

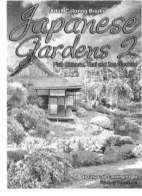

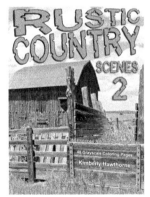

@Life Escapes Grayscale Adult Coloring Books   Look at Me Looking at You By Laura Kilgore

   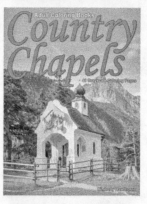 

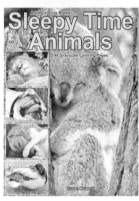    

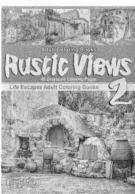    

https://coloringbooksforadults.shop

NOTICE

Photos used in the production of this book were photographed and grayscaled by Laura Kilgore, a member of Life Escapes Grayscale Adult Coloring Books

To speak with Laura, use email: kilgore7098@gmail.com

Disclaimer: All original artwork provided digitally is protected via a watermark of Life Escapes logo. This watermark doesn't mean we claim credit for original artwork. It is to protect the original artists which are largely unknown to us. When we know who the original artist is, we place the info below the coloring page.

With that being said, we give our customers personal use rights to our grayscaled coloring pages.

Personal use means you can make copies of uncolored images/pages in print or digital format from this book for your own personal use, but you cannot distribute them in any way without written permission from Life Escapes Adult Coloring Books owner - Kimberly Hawthorne and/or partnering designer

Not Permitted

Any and all uncolored images/pages as they appear in print, pdf, digital download and on website (http://coloringbooksforadults.shop)
Exception: free coloring pages offered on website and social media can be shared freely online when linking back to any page on coloringbooksforadults.shop.
You may NOT share coupon codes or links for digital downloads.

For questions, comments or other...please contact us at
life.escapes.series@gmail.com

https://coloringbooksforadults.shop

CPSIA information can be obtained
at www.ICGtesting.com
Printed in the USA
LVHW061103140123
737171LV00013BB/746